Harmonia Sacra:
OR,
DIVINE HYMNS
AND
DIALOGUES:
WITH
A THROUGH-BASS for the *Theorbo-Lute*, *Bass-Viol*, *Harpsichord*, or *Organ*.

Composed by the Best Masters of the last and Present Age.

The WORDS by several Learned and Pious Persons.

The First BOOK. The 3d. Edition very much Enlarg'd and Corrected; also Four Excellent Anthems of the late Mr. *H. Purcell's*, never before Printed.

Cannon a 3, in the Fifth and Eighth below, rising a Note every time.

[musical notation]

Laudate Dominum de Cœ—lis, lau—da——te eum in ex—cel—sis.

Where Musick and Devotion joyn,	No longer do we pass,
The Way to *Canaan* pleasant is;	Thro' a dry Barren Wilderness;
We travel on with Songs Divine,	But thro' a Land where Milk and Honey flow,
Ravish'd with Sacred Extasies.	The Paths to Heav'n above leads thro' a Heav'n (below.

LONDON:

Printed by *William Pearson*, for *S. H.* and Sold by *John Young*, Musical-Instrument-Seller, at the Dolphin and Crown in St. *Paul's* Church-Yard. 1716.

Where may be had, *Simpson's Compendium*.

Henry Purcell et al.

Harmonia Sacra or Divine Hymns and Dialogues
The First Book

First published by John Young in 1726.

Republished by Travis & Emery 2008.

Published by
Travis & Emery Music Bookshop
17 Cecil Court, London, WC2N 4EZ, United Kingdom.
(+44) 20 7240 2129
neworders@travis-and-emery.com

Hardback: ISBN10: 1-904331-59-9   ISBN13: 978-1904331-59-9
Paperback: ISBN10: 1-904331-60-2   ISBN13: 978-1904331-60-2

Harmonia Sacra:
OR,
DIVINE HYMNS
AND
DIALOGUES:
WITH
A THROUGH-BASS for the *Theorbo-Lute*, *Bass-Viol*, *Harpsichord*, or *Organ*.

Composed by the Best Masters of the last and Present Age.

The Words by several Learned and Pious Persons.

The First BOOK. The 3d. Edition very much Enlarg'd and Corrected; also Four Excellent Anthems of the late Mr. *H. Purcell*'s, never before Printed.

Cannon a 3, in the Fifth and Eighth below, rising a Note every time.

Laudate Dominum de Cœ—lis, lau—da——te eum in ex—cel—sis.

Where Musick and Devotion joyn, The Way to *Canaan* pleasant is; We travel on with Songs Divine, Ravish'd with Sacred Extasies.	No longer do we pass, Thro' a dry Barren Wilderness; But thro' a Land where Milk and Honey flow, The Paths to Heav'n above leads thro' a Heav'n (below.

LONDON:

Printed by *William Pearson*, for *S. H.* and Sold by *John Young*, Musical-Instrument-Seller, at the Dolphin and Crown in St. *Paul*'s Church-Yard. 1726.

Where may be had, *Simpson's Compendium*.

To the QUEEN's MOST Excellent Majesty:

MADAM,

THE Best of Authors have been always Presents for the Best of Princes, and it would have been a great breach of Duty in me, to lay these Excellent Performances any where but at Your Majesty's Sacred Feet. Your Majesty has a double Right to their Patronage, from Your Love to Musick, and affection to Devotion, and as You are an Encourager of Both, so both apply themselves with all Humility for Your Protection.

Your Majesty was pleased to give Mr Purcell Your Royal Approbation when Living, and it is Humbly hop'd the Memory of him will not be unpleasing to You now He is Dead; and though the Publisher has no Merit in himself to Recommend Him to Your Majesty's Presence, Your Majesty will Graciously receive what begs Your Acceptance, for the sake of those Ingenious Gentlemen that Oblig'd the World with these Compositions.

The Encouragement of Arts and Sciences is one of the Prerogatives of Royalty, and the most Glorious Reigns have allways had the Reputation of being the most Learned. What may we not then expect under Your Majesty's Auspicious Government? This makes me presume to hope, that the Piety of the Words, and Artfulness of the Musick, will not appear undeserving of Your Majesty's Favour. Which if they may be so Happy as to obtain I shall think it my Glory to continue my great cost and Pains in contributing to the Publick satisfaction, and ever make it my endeavour to approve my self, Madam,

Your Majesty's most Dutyful,

Most Devoted, and most

Faithful Subject

HENRY PLAYFORD.

TO THE
READER.

THE Youthful and Gay have already been entertain'd with variety of Rare Compositions, where the lighter Sportings of Wit have been Tun'd by the most Artful Hands, and made at once to gratify a Delicate Ear, and a wanton Curiosity.

I now therefore address to others, who are no less *Musical*, though they are more *Devout*. There are many Pious Persons, who are not only just Admirers, but excellent Judges too, both of *Musick* and *Wit*; to these a singular Regard is due, and their exquisite Relish of the former ought not to be pall'd by an unagreeable Composition of the later. Divine *Hymns* are therefore the most proper Entertainment for them, which, as they make the sweetest, and indeed the only, Melowdy to a *Religious Ear*, so are they in themselves the very Glory and Perfection of *Musick*.

For 'tis the meanest and most Mechanical Office of this *Noble Science* to play upon the Ear, and strike the Fancy with a superficial Delight; but when Holy and Spiritual Things are its Subject, it proves of a more subtile and refined Nature, whilst darting it self through the Organs of Sense, it warms and actuates all the Powers of the Soul, and fills the Mind with the brightest and most ravishing Contemplation. *Musick* and *Poetry* have in all Ages been accounted Divine, and therefore they cannot be more naturally employed, than when they are conversant about *Heaven*, that Region of *Harmony*, from wence they are derived.

Now as to this present Collection, I need said no more than that the *Words* were penn'd by such Persons, as are, and have been very Eminet both for Learning and Piety; and indeed, he that reads them as he ought, will soon find his Affections warm'd, as with a Coal from the Altar, and feel the Breathings of Devine Love from every Line. Here therefore the *Musical* and *Devout* cannot want Matter both to exercise there Skill, and heighten their Devotion; to which excellent Porposes that these two Books may be truly effectual, is the hearty desire of

Your humble Servant,

Henry Playford

A Table of the Divine HYMNS and DIALOGUES contain'd in this Book.

A
Awake, awake and with attention hear, Page 13
And art thou griev'd, sweet and sacred Dove! 25

C
Come honest Sexton, take thy Spade, 5
Close thine Eyes, and sleep secure, thy Soul is safe, 41

E
Enough my Muse of Earthly things, and Inspirations but of Winds, 31

G
Great God and Just! 60

H
How art thou fall'n, from Heav'n O Lucifer! 27
How long great God, how long must I, 33
Hark how the wakeful cheerful Cock a Diologue, 44
Help, Father Abraham, help a Dialogue, 49
How have I stray'd, my God, 57
Happy the man, to whom the sacred Muse, 73

I
In the black dismal Dungeon of Despair, Page 7
I know that my Redemer Lives, 39

L
Let the Night perish, 10
Lord, I have sin'd 37

N
Now, that the Sun hath veil'd his Light, 1

O
O that mine Eyes wou'd melt into a flood, 64
O the sad Day, 66
O God for ever Blest, 69

P
Peaceful is he and most secure, 55

T
The Earth trembled, 3
Thou wakeful Shepherd, 6
Thus Mortals must submit to Fate, 36

W
With sick and famish'd Eyes, 22
We sing to him whose Wisdom form'd the Ear, 63
Wilt thou forgive that Sin, 67

The four following Anthems by Mr. *H. Purcell.*

Blessed is he that considereth the Poor, Psal. 41, v. 31   Page 91
I was glad when they said unto me, Psal. 122 the 7 1st. verses, 98
O give thanks unto the Lord, Psal. 106 the 4 1st. verses, 106
My Song shall be always of the Loving kindness of the Lord, Psal. 89. 121

ADVERTISEMENT.

Miscellanea Sacra, or Divine Poems, Collected by *N. Tate* Esq; The second Edition, containing most of the Words in this first and second Books of *Harmonia Sacra.* Price bound two Shillings Printed for *Henry Playford,* where is also to be had the most Excellent Tragedy of *King Saul,* Written by a Deceased Person of Honour. Price One Shilling Sixpence.

[1]

Harmonia Sacra, &c.

The First BOOK.

An EVENING HYMN.

On a Ground. *Words by Dr.* William Fuller, *late Lord-Bishop of* Lincoln. Mr. *Henry Purcell.*

Ow, now that the Sun hath veil'd his Light, and bid the World good night; to the soft Bed, to the soft, the soft Bed my Body I dispose, but where, where shall my Soul repose? Dear, dear God, even in thy Arms, ev'n in thy Arms, and can there be a—ny so swee———t Se—cu—ri—ty! Can there be, a—ny so sweet, so sweet Se—cu—ri—ty!

B

BOOK I.   Harmonia Sacra.   3

—lu-jab, Hal— — — — — — — — —lelujab, Halle-lujab, Hallelujab, Halle—

—lu-jab, Hal— — — — — — — — —le—lu—

—jab, Hal— — — — —le—lu—jab.

On our Saviour's Passion.   Mr *Henry Purcell.*

THe Earth trembled, and Heav'ns clos'd Eye, was loth to see the Lord of Glo---ry dye; The Sky was clad in Mourning, and the Spheres for--get their Har---mo—ny, the Clouds drop'd Tears: Th'ambitious Dead a——

BOOK I. Harmonia Sacra.

The PASSING-BELL. *Set by Mr.* Matthew Lock.

Come, honest *Sexton*, take thy Spade, and let my Grave be quickly made;
Thou still art ready for the Dead, like a kind Host to make a Bed: I now am come to
be thy Guest, let me in some dark Lodging rest; for I am weary, full of pain, and
of my Pilgrimage complain: On Heav'n's Decree I waiting lye, and all my Wishes are to die.

CHORUS.

Hark! hark! I hear my Passing Bell, I hear my Passing Bell, farewell, farewell, my loving Friends, farewell.

Hark! hark! I hear my Passing Bell, I hear my Passing Bell, farewell, farewell, my loving Friends, farewell.

Make my cold Bed (good *Sexton!*) deep,
That my poor Bones safely sleep;
Until that sad and joyful day,
When from above a Voice shall say,
'Wake all ye Dead, lift up your Eyes,
The Great Creator bids you rise!

Then do I hope, among the Just,
To shake off this polluted Dust;
And with new Robes of Glory drest,
To have Access among the Blest.

Chorus. *Hark! hark!* &c.

Harmonia Sacra. BOOK I.

A MORNING HYMN.

Words by Dr. William Fuller, *late Lord Bishop of* Lincoln. *Set by Mr.* Henry Purcell.

Thou wakefull Shepherd, that does If—rael keep, rais'd by thy Goodness from the Bed of Sleep; to thee I offer up this Hymn, as my best Morning Sacrifice, may it be gracious, may it be gracious in thine Eyes, to raise me from the Bed of Sin: And do I live to see a—-no-ther day, I vow, my God, I vow henceforth to walk thy ways, and fi- - - - - - - - - - - - - -ng thy Praise, all those few days thou shalt allow.

Could I re—deem the Time I have mispent, in sin--full Merriment; could I un-—

BOOK I. Harmonia Sacra. 7

*Words by Dr. William Fuller, *late Lord Bishop of* Lincoln.   *Set by Mr.* Henry Purcell.

Harmonia Sacra. BOOK I.

JOB's *Curse, Translated by* Dr. Taylor *Bishop of* Down *in* Ireland.

Set by Mr. Henry Purcell.

LET the Night perish, cur—sed be the Morn', wherein 'twas said, There is a Manchild born! Let not the Lord regard that day, but shrowd its fa———tal Glory in some sul—len Cloud: May the dark Shades of an E—ter—nal Night, exclude the least kind Beam of downing Light; let unborn Babes, as in the Womb they lye, if it be mention'd, give a Groan and dye: No sounds of Joy therein shall charm the Ear; no Sun, no Moon, no twilight Stars appear; but a thick Vale of gloo———my Darkness wear. Why

BOOK I. Harmonia Sacra. 11

BOOK I.   Harmonia Sacra.   13

The 34th. Chapter of Isaiah Paraphras'd by Mr. Cowley.
Set by Mr. Henry Purcell.

16   Harmonia Sacra.   BOOK I.

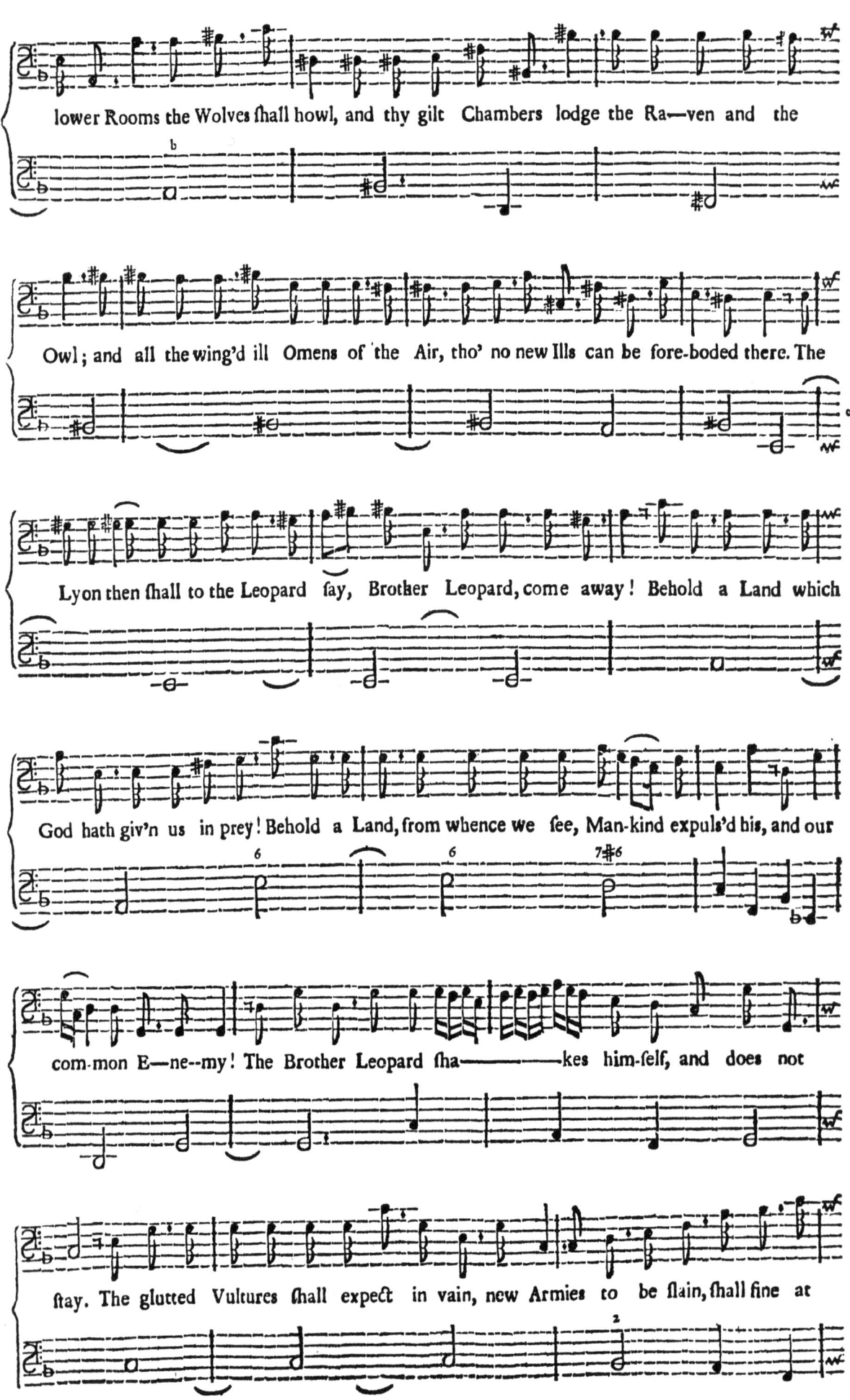

BOOK I. Harmonia Sacra. 21

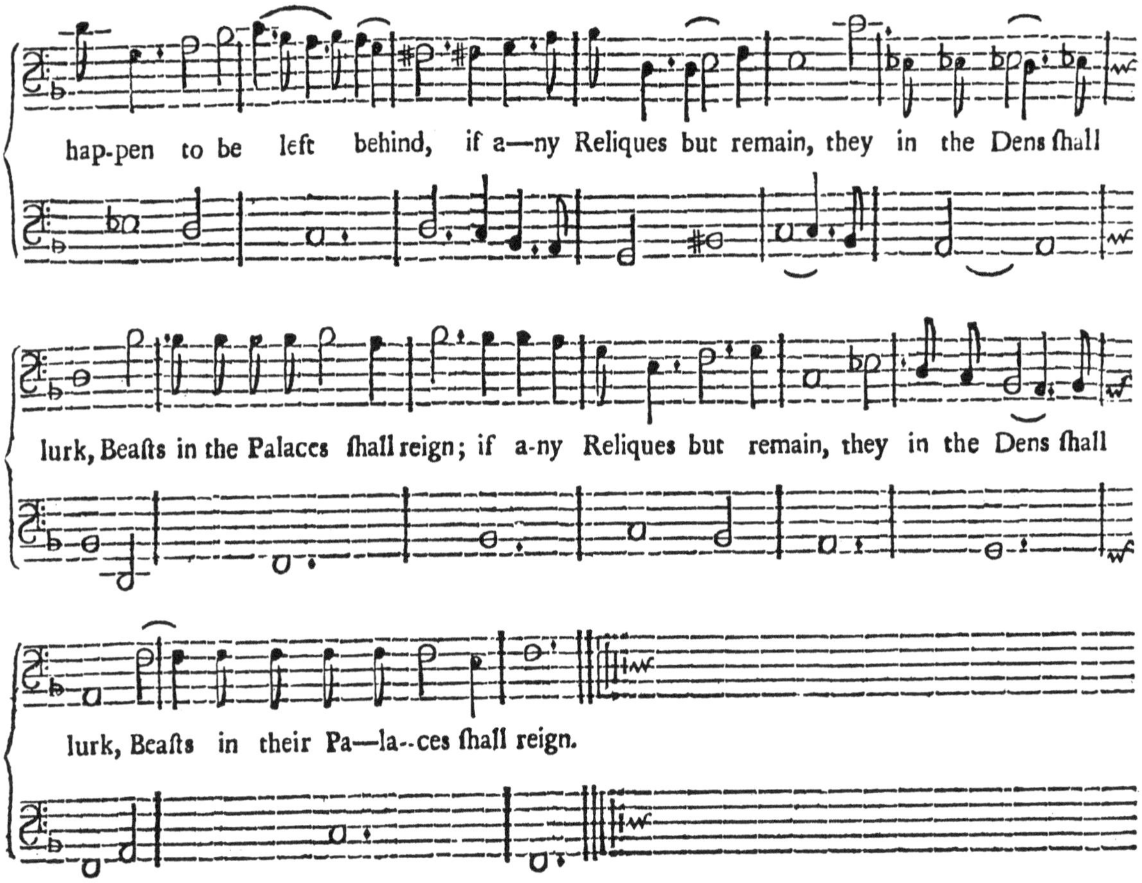

22   Harmonia Sacra.   BOOK I.

hap-pen to be left behind, if a—ny Reliques but remain, they in the Dens shall

lurk, Beasts in the Palaces shall reign; if a-ny Reliques but remain, they in the Dens shall

lurk, Beasts in their Pa—la--ces shall reign.

Words by Mr. Herbert, *Set by* Mr. Henry Purcell.

With sick and famish'd Eyes, with dou————bling Knees, and weary Bones, to thee my Cries, to thee my Groans, to thee my Sighs, my Tears ascend, no end; my Throat, my Soul is hoarse, my Heart is wither'd, like a Ground which

BOOK I. Harmonia Sacra. 23

Harmonia Sacra.

25

Words by Mr. George Herbert, in his Church-Poems.

Set by Dr. John Blow.

And art thou griev'd, sweet and sacred Dove, when I am sour, and cross thy Love! Griev'd for me, the God of Strength and Pow'r; griev'd for a Worm, which when I tread, I pass a-way, and leave it dead. Then weep, mine Eyes, the God of Love doth grieve, weep, foolish Heart, and weep-ing live; for Death is dry as Dust; yet if ye part, end as the Night, whose sable Hew your Sins express, melt in to Dew: When sawcy Mirth shall knock, or call at Door, cry out, Get hence, or cry no more; Al--mighty

Yet if I wail not still, since still to wail, Natures denies, and Flesh would fail, if my Deserts were Masters of mine Eyes. Lord, pardon, for thy Son makes good my want of Tears, my want of Tears, with store of Blood.

Lucifer's *Fawl.* Set by Dr. John Blow.

HOW art thou fall'n from Heav'n, O Lu-ci-fer! How art thou fall'n from Heav'n, O Lu-ci-fer! How art thou fall'n from Heav'n,

BOOK I.   Harmonia Sacra.   29

BOOK I. Harmonia Sacra. 31

BOOK I. Harmonia Sacra. 33

Spirits above, with all their Com——ments can explain, how all the whole Worlds
Spirits above, with all their Comments can explain, how all the whole Worlds
Life to dy————e, did not disdain.
Life to dy————e, did not disdain.

The Aspiration. *The Words by Mr.* Norris, *of* Wadham Colledge Oxon.
Set by Mr. *Henry Purcell.*

Ow long, how long, grea———t God, how long must I, im———
—mur'd in this dork Pri—son lye? Where at the Grates, and A—ve-nues of Sence, my Soul must
watch to have in--tel——li—gence; where but faint Gleams of thee sa—-lute my Sight,

BOOK I. Harmonia Sacra. 35

Harmonia Sacra.
BOOK I.

Sett by Dr. William Turner.

Thus Mortals must submit to Fate, some more ear—ly, some more late; Life to the World is on—ly lent, and is re--pay'd by Time and Ac---ci-dent, and is re--pay'd by Time and Ac--ci—dent: Why then should wretched Souls repine, for be—ing soonest made Divine; and go where they shall be se--cure of Joys, and no more shock of Chance endure? There Joys are perfect, and no Care, nothing is left to wish or fear; there Joys are perfect, and no Care, nothing is left to wish or fear.

BOOK I.　　　Harmonia Sacra.　　　37

CHORUS.

How hap-py, how hap-py's the Soul that has took his best flight, from Darkness to

How hap-py's the Soul, &c.

Light, from be—low to a-bove, from Envy and Hatred, to Praise and to Love, from Envy and

Hatred, from Envy and Hatred to Praise and to Love.

Words by Dr. Jeremiah Taylor.　　*Set by* Mr. Pelham Humphryes.

Lord! I have sinn'd, I have sinn'd, and the black Number swells

to such a dis—mal Sum, that should my sto—ny Heart, and Eyes, and this whole

sin—ful Trunk a Flood become, and ru———————n to Tears, their

BOOK I. Harmonia Sacra. 39

Words by Sir Thomas Dereham. *Set by Mr.* Matthew Lock.

40 Harmonia Sacra. BOOK I.

BOOK I.   Harmonia Sacra.   41

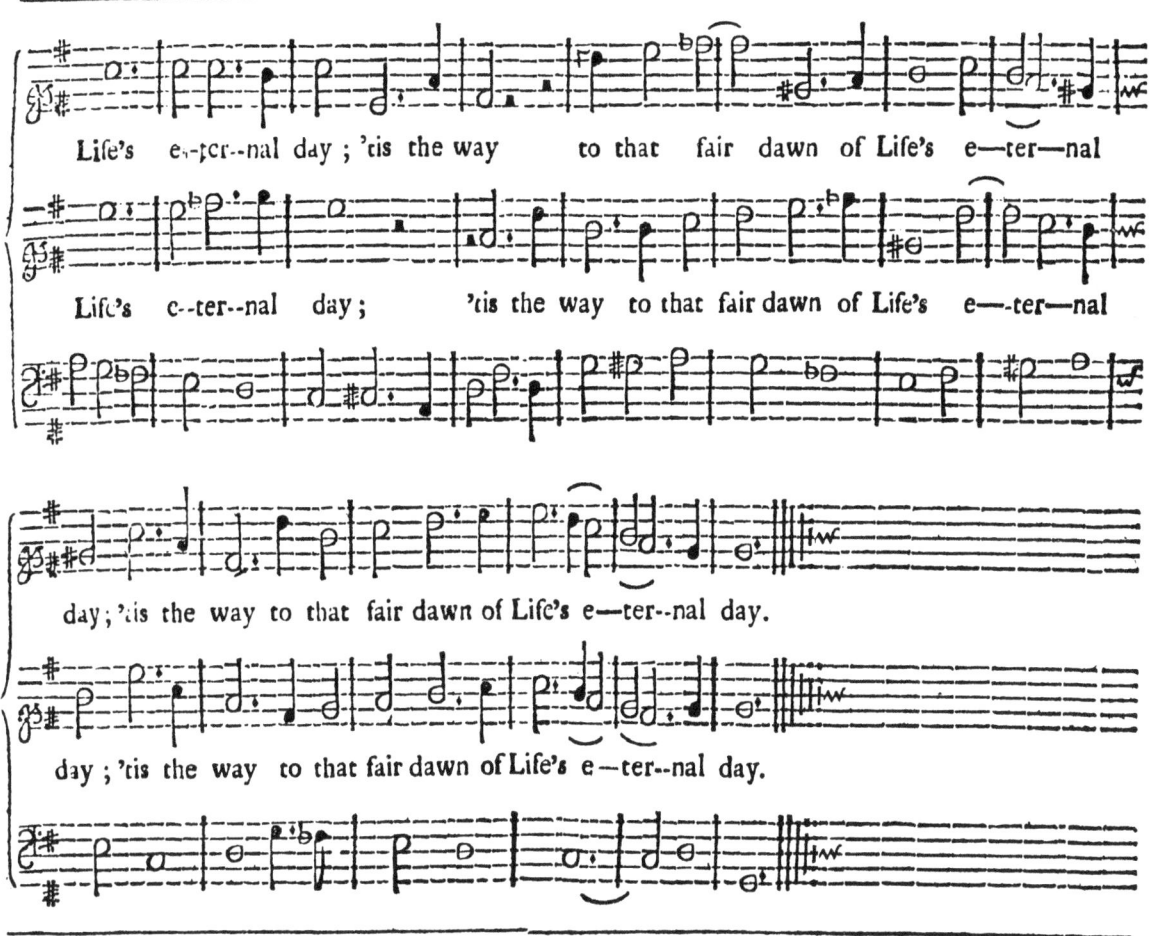

Upon a Quiet Conscience, by *King* Charles *the* I. *of Blessed Memory.*
Set by *Mr.* Henry Purcell.

M

Harmonia Sacra. BOOK I.

A Dialogue between two Penitents.

First Penitent.   Set by Mr. Pelham Humphryes, *and* Dr. John Blow.

Hark! how the wakeful chearful Cock, the Villagers A—stro--lo--ger and Clock, clapping his Wings, proclaims the Day, and chides thy Sleep and Night away! I hear, and thank my kind Remembrancer, he wakes a Sin, that slept within, rouzes a Crime that be—fore whuld not stir: Flow, flow my Tears! O when will you be—gin! Saint Peter's Bird reproves Saint Peter's Sin! Complaining Man! Hast thou thy Christ deny'd!

Second Penitent. Wo's me! Wo's me! I have, more than Saint Pe-ter did, with less excuse, and many

BOOK I.   Harmonia Sacra.   49

A Dialogue betwixt Dives and Abraham.

Dives.   Set by Dr. *John Blow.*

Help, help, Father A—bram! Help, for Mercy's sake! Be-—hold my Torments, for Mercy's sake! Behold my Tor——ments in—————this burning Lake! Send *La—za—rus* with Whirl—————winds, that he may these flakes of mel—————ting Sul—phur fan a—way.

Abraham.

What Son of Hell and Darkness dare molest this blessed Saint, scarce warm yet on my Breast?

Dives.

'Tis I, 'tis I great *Mammon's* e—-qual once, whose Lott is on—ly, on———ly *Tophet*

BOOK I.   Harmonia Sacra.   53

BOOK I.   Harmonia Sacra.   55

Words by Mr. Tho. Flatman.   Set by Dr. *John Blow.*

Peaceful is he, and most se—cure, whose Heart and Actions all are pure; how smooth and pleasant is his way, whilst Life's *Meander* slides away!

If a fierce Thunderbolt does fly, this Man can un-concerned lye: Know 'tis not levell'd at his Head, so nei—ther Noise nor Flash can dread; though a swift Whirlwind tear in sunder, Heav'n above him, or Earth under; tho' the Rocks on heaps do tum——ble, or the World to A—shes crumble; tho' the stu--pen-dious Mountains from on high, drop

BOOK I.   Harmonia Sacra.   57

The Words by Dr. Fuller, *late Lord-Bishop of* Lincoln.
Set by Mr. Henry Purcell.

BOOK I. Harmonia Sacra. 59

60   Harmonia Sacra.   BOOK I.

A Penitential HYMN.   Set by Mr. *Henry Purcell*.

Great God, and Just! How can'st thou see, dear God, our Mi--se--ry, and not in Mercy set us free? Poor, mi-se-ra-ble Man! How wer't thou born? Weak as the dewy Jewels of the Morn'! Wrapt up in ten--der Dust, guarded with Sins and Lust; who, like Court-Flatterers, wait, to serve themselves in thy unhappy Fate: Wealth is a Snare, and Po-ver--ty brings in Inlets for Theft, paving the way for Sin; each perfum'd Va--ni--ty doth gent-ly breath Sin in thy Soul, and whispers it to

BOOK I. Harmonia Sacra. 63

Set by Mr. *Henry Purcell.*

WE sing to him, whose Wisdom form'd the Ear, our Songs, let him who gave us Voices, hear; we joy in God, who is the Spring of Mirth, who loves the Harmo--ny of Heav'n and Earth; our humble Sonnets shall That Praise rehearse, who is the Musick of the Universe.

CHORUS.

And whilst we sing, and whilst we sing, we con——secrate our Art, and offer up with ev'ry Tongue a Heart; and whilst we sing, and whilst we sing, we con——secrate our Art, and offer up, and offer up, with ev'—ry Tongue a Heart.

And whilst we sing, and whilst we sing, we con——se—crate our Art, and offer up with ev'ry Tongue a Heart; and whilst we sing, whilst we sing, we con——secrate our Art, and offer, and offer up, offer up, with ev'—ry Tongue a Heart.

64　　　　　　Harmonia Sacra.　　　　　BOOK I.

Set by Dr. *John Blow.*

Harmonia Sacra. BOOK I.

On a Dying-Friend. The Words by Mr. Tho. Flatman.
Set by Mr. *Pelham Humphreys.*

OH the sad day! when Friends shall shake their heads, and say of mise-rable me, Hark how he groans! look how he pants for Breath! see, see, how he struggles with the Pangs of Death! When they shall say of these dear Eyes, How hollow, and how dim they be! Mark how his Breast does swell and rise, against his potent E—nemies. When some old Friend shall step to my Bed--side, touch my chill Face, and thence shall gent--ly slide; and when his next Com--panions say, How does he do? What hopes? Shall turn a--way, an--swe-ring on—ly with a

BOOK I.   Harmonia Sacra.   67

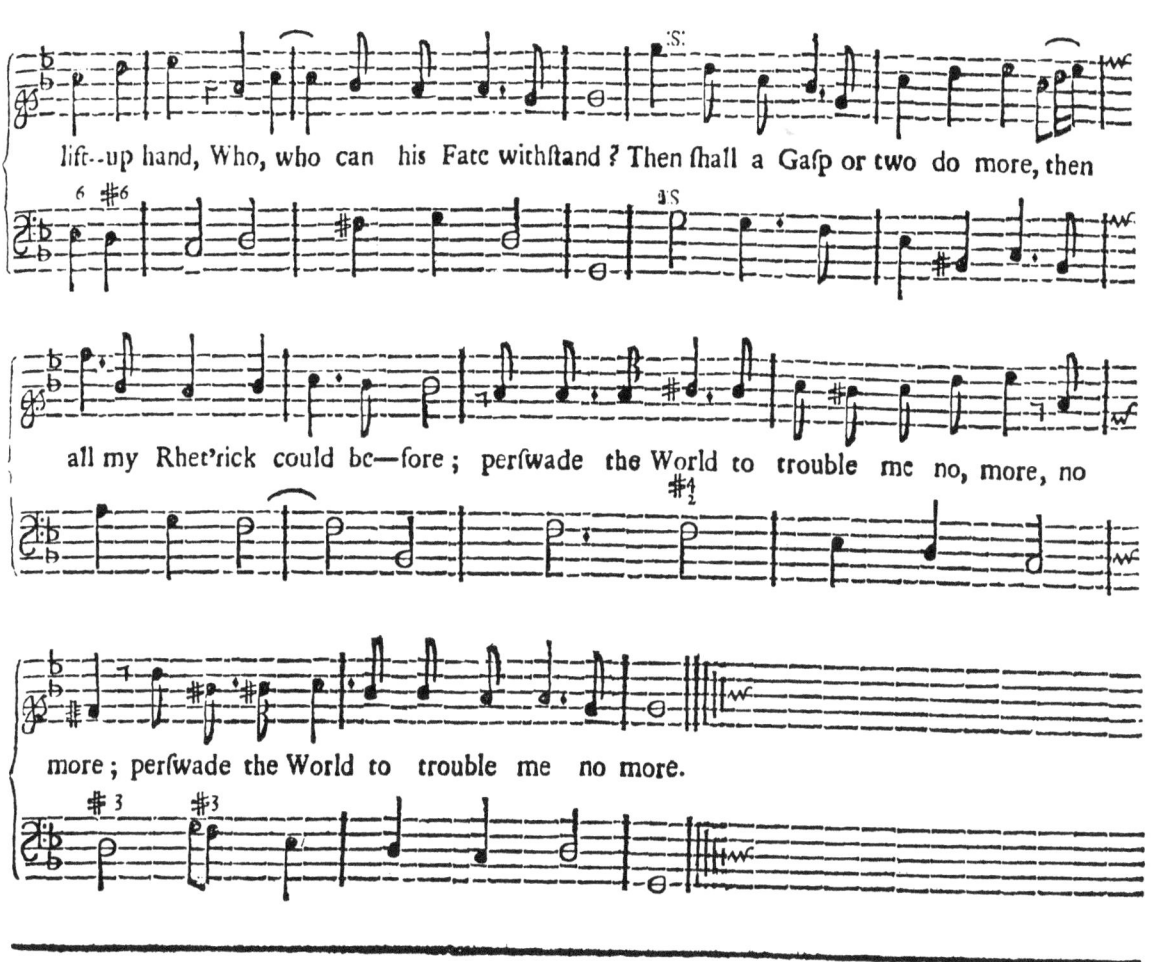

lift-up hand, Who, who can his Fate withstand? Then shall a Gasp or two do more, then all my Rhet'rick could be—fore; perswade the World to trouble me no, more, no more; perswade the World to trouble me no more.

The Words by Dr. Dunn.   *Set by Mr.* Pelham Humphryes.

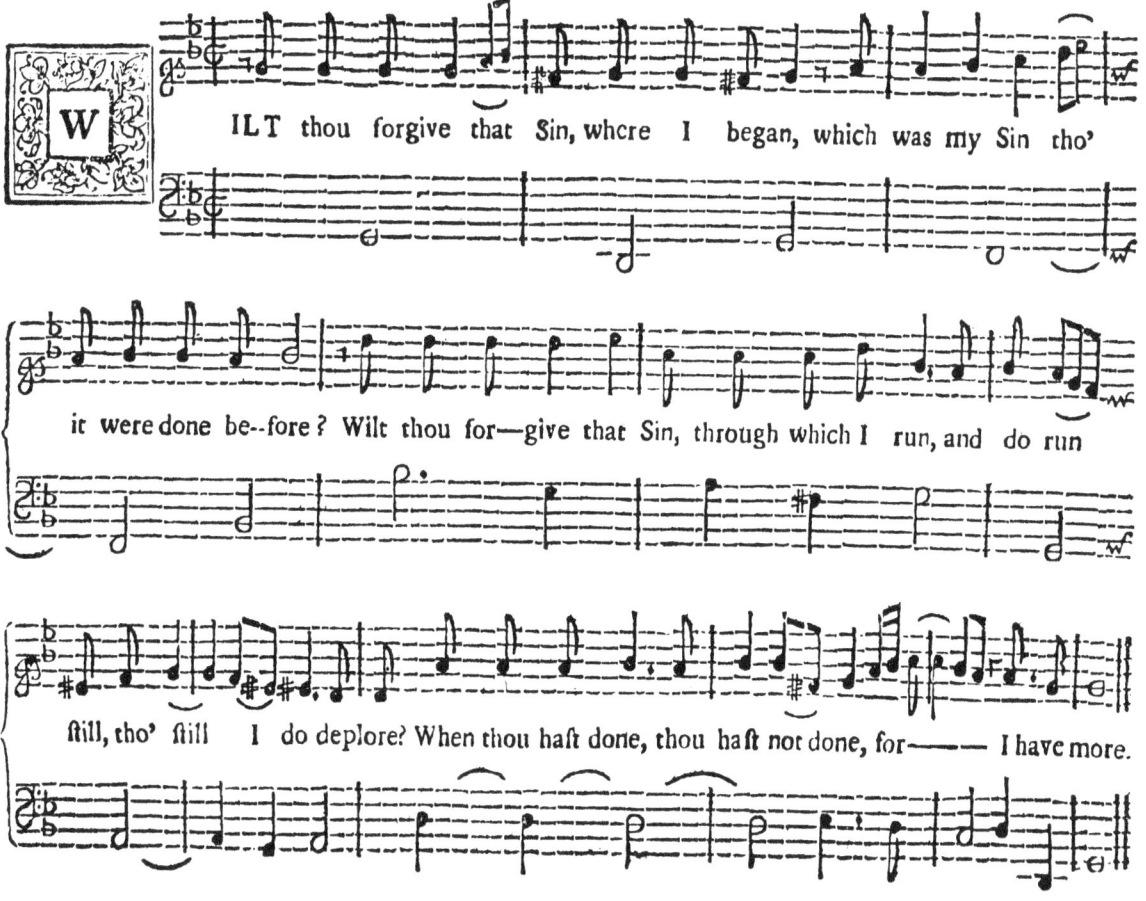

WILT thou forgive that Sin, where I began, which was my Sin tho' it were done be--fore? Wilt thou for—give that Sin, through which I run, and do run still, tho' still I do deplore? When thou hast done, thou hast not done, for —— I have more.

BOOK I. Harmonia Sacra. 69

A Divine HYMN. *Sett by Mr.* John Church.

God for ever bleſt in bound——leſs peace & reſt, whoſe habi-——tation is in light refin'd, look from thy bright and glo-——rious Throne with pi-ty, with pity and compaſſion look, look down behold and ea-——ſe my troubled mind, pain and diſtraction from my heart remove, thou God of Conſolation, thou God of Conſolation and of Love: And thou who ſets at the right hand of Bliſs, the Spring of all true Jo————y and hapineſs, who when thou had'ſt reſign'd the

Harmonia Sacra. 73

The DISSOLUTION. Sett by Mr. John Weldon.

Happy, happy the Man to whom the Sacred Muse her nightly visits pays, and with her magick Rod Opens his mortal Eyes, he, he Nature at one glance surveys, and past and future near and distant views. I'm mounted on Fancy, and long to be gone, I'm mounted on Fancy, and long to be gone to some Age, or some World, to some Age or some World unknown.

BOOK I. Harmonia Sacra. 75

82 Harmonia Sacra. BOOK I.

BOOK I.   Harmonia Sacra.   85

BOOK I.   Harmonia Sacra.   89

90 Harmonia Sacra. BOOK I.

BOOK I.   Harmonia Sacra.   91

The following ANTHEMS, *by the late Mr.* Henry Purcell.

BOOK I.   Harmonia Sacra.   95

BOOK I. Harmonia Sacra. 97

Harmonia Sacra. BOOK I.

An ANTHEM, *by the late Mr.* Henry Purcell.

BOOK I.   Harmonia Sacra.   99

BOOK I.   Harmonia Sacra.   101

BOOK I.   Harmonia Sacra.   103

BOOK I. Harmonia Sacra. 105

Harmonia Sacra. BOOK I.

An ANTHEM, *by the late Mr.* Henry Purcell.

108   Harmonia Sacra.   BOOK I.

110 Harmonia Sacra. BOOK I.

BOOK I.   Harmonia Sacra.   113

G g

BOOK I.   Harmonia Sacra.   115

BOOK I. Harmonia Sacra. 117

BOOK I.   Harmonia Sacra.   119

Harmonia Sacra. BOOK I.

BOOK I.   Harmonia Sacra.   121

An ANTHEM, *by the late* Mr. Henry Purcell.

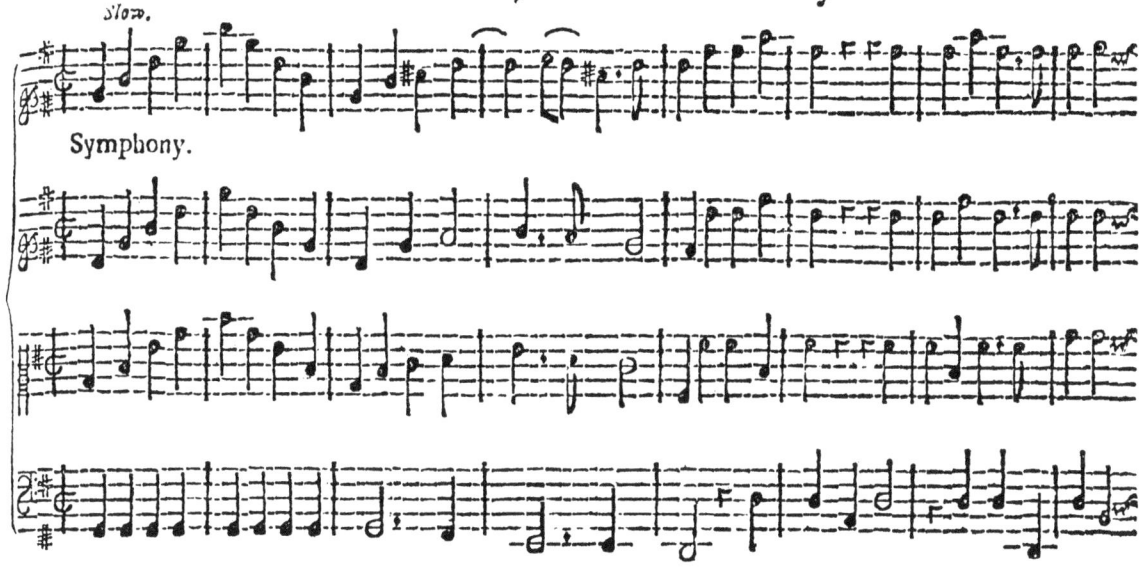

Symphony.

—drous works, and thy truth in the Congregation of the Saints; and thy

truth in the Congregation of the Saints; For who is

he among the Clouds that shall be compar'd unto the Lord? For who is he among the

Clouds that shall be compar'd unto the Lord? For who is he, for who is he among the

Clouds that shall be compar'd unto the Lord? And what is he, what, what is he, is he among the

Gods that shall be like unto the Lord? and what is he, what, what is he among the

FINIS.

www.ingramcontent.com/pod-product-compliance
Lightning Source LLC
Chambersburg PA
CBHW081602040426
42451CB00016B/3452